# THE COUNTRY
## PRESERVES COMPANION

# THE COUNTRY
# PRESERVES COMPANION

## JOCASTA INNES
## PHOTOGRAPHY BY JAMES MERRELL

CollinsPublishersSanFrancisco
*A Division of* HarperCollins*Publishers*

# The Country Preserves Companion
*Jocasta Innes*

First published in USA in 1995
by Collins Publishers San Francisco
1160 Battery Street, San Francisco CA 94111

First published in Great Britain in 1995 by Mitchell Beazley
an imprint of Reed Consumer Books Limited

Photography by *James Merrell*
Illustrations by *Michael Hill*

Art Editor *Peta Waddington*        Art Director *Jacqui Small*
Editors *Sophie Pearse*             Production *Heather O'Connell*
    and *Jonathan Hilton*    Executive Editor *Judith More*

Library of Congress Cataloging-in-Publication Data
Innes, Jocasta
  The country preserves companion/Jocasta Innes: photography by James Merrell.
    p. cm.
  Includes index.
  ISBN 0-00-255493-3
  1. Canning and preserving. I. Title.
TX603. I56  1995
641.4'2--dc20
                       94-37068
                       CIP

Colour reproduction by Rival Colour, UK
Produced by Mandarin Offset
Printed and bound in China

# CONTENTS

# INTRODUCTION

The art of preserving good fresh food is at least as old as the art of cookery itself — of which, of course, it is a noble branch. Until very recent times a glance into any larder would have told a satisfying tale of thrifty labors — of subtle blends of spice and fruits; of steaming pots, and brimming ladles; of a kitchen garden carefully tended; and of pleasant trips into the countryside in the spring and fall, basket in hand, to gather mushrooms and berries — the ranks of bottles and jars twinkling with promise of imminent reward.

In an age when a lot of food can be simply stuffed into a freezer, you might ask whether making preserves is worth the trouble. Food comes out of the freezer as it went in, and mostly still needs cooking; preserves, on the other hand, may mellow and ripen over the months, and emerge ready to eat. What is really preserved, in bottles and jars and stoneware crocks, under airtight lids, is wonderful country cooking, its pleasures heightened by being deferred.

The subtle changes to the raw ingredients used in the recipes in this book cannot be achieved in any other way. You can freeze an orange, certainly, but all you get is a sorry, soggy fruit: but in a freshly opened jar of homemade marmalade you have something rich and rare.

# THE PRESERVES KITCHEN

# EQUIPMENT

Some of the recipes in this book require next to no specialized equipment, and even for the jams a heavy-bottomed saucepan and a wooden spoon may be adequate. But if you are planning to cook in any quantity, you will find it useful to invest in a large preserving pan, with a handle and pouring lip, containing anything between 1½ and 2 gallons. This may seem more than you could manage, but it is a good idea to keep the pan only half-full, at the most; otherwise boiling sugar can foam and overflow in a moment. Preserving pans are relatively wide and shallow, to help evaporation, and shelve gradually outward toward the lip, like buckets. The best preserving pans are made of heavy-gauge stainless steel, with a really heavy bottom to spread the heat; and they are expensive. You can find less expensive versions, down to enameled iron and non-stick aluminum, but the internal coating must be perfect. Plain aluminum should be avoided; and old copper or brass pans, are no good for pickles: the vinegar will leach out the metallic salts and flavor the preserve horribly.

A set of scales is useful and you will certainly need a battery of wooden spoons, preferably cut on the slant for stirring the bottom of the pan, with long handles to keep your fingers away from boiling sugar as it bubbles and heaves.

To tell, infallibly, when the jam is set, a jam-making thermometer is very useful, as are a wide-spouted jam funnel and a jug for transferring the scalding produce into the jars without spills or tears. You will need a fine nylon or stainless steel strainer, a stainless steel or enamelled strainer, and a lemon squeezer. Sooner or later you will want cheesecloth for straining jellies, and for keeping herbs and spices, pips and peel, separate from the mixture in your pan. If you can find prefabricated jelly bags sold in some kitchenware stores, they do the job without fiddle.

Of course you need a chopping board — the bigger the better. Boards for carving roasts, with a gutter around the edge for catching the juices, are ideal. Plastic or vinyl boards are clean, and very light; but you may prefer, as I do, a thick wooden board with some feel to it, and to sweep the fruit off it into a pan held underneath.

Nothing beats the knife you like, as long as it is sharp. Itinerant chefs carry their own around with them, and once you have a knife that suits you, hang on to it. It should preferably be stainless steel, and the better quality stainless knives will take sharpening with a steel or whetstone, so that they cut swiftly and cleanly, without pulling or ragged edges. Food

processors can be used to save time, but be warned: they will not do much for either the texture or appearance of your preserves. Most preserves will keep for months or even years: a few extra minutes at the start with a knife and board are worthwhile.

A paring knife comes in handy for peeling apples by the pound. An apple coring device saves time, too, although if your apples are very large you should check that it has done the job properly. The paring knife will also zest lemons but a small steel kitchen knife is sharper and more satisfying to use, leaving the pith behind.

The choice of containers for your preserves is up to you: the only criterion is that the seal should be perfect. Old jam jars, new jars with clip-down rubber sealing rings, stoneware crocks, all will do; but unless your family is very large, 1-pint containers are the most suitable size. You will need waxed paper, elastic bands and labels, all of which you can buy in a single package. Unless you really enjoy cleaning up, a pile of old newspapers, for spreading almost everywhere, is invaluable. And if all this sounds daunting, remember that our forbears made do with earthen crocks, wooden spoons, and an iron pan!

One last thought: never be afraid of making too much. Most of the recipes in this book provide for a decent amount — say 6 to 8 jars; but preserves dealt with glut, and were intended to be made on a grand scale. Provided you have the jars and a big enough pan, making more jam does not mean more complication. You are filling jars and bottles with good things that will keep, in some cases, for years, and if you can't eat them all, friends and relatives probably will.

# BOTTLING TECHNIQUES

Jars and bottles, and their lids and corks too, should be scrupulously clean: wash them in warm soapy water, rinse, then boil for half an hour and finally dry them off in a preheated oven at 225°F for 30 minutes, or until dry. Cheesecloth should be scalded before use.

Jams and jellies, chutneys and pickles, should all be sealed when either hot or cold, but never when tepid. Fill the jars to within ¼ inch of the rim. Place a circle of waxed paper on the surface of the jam, smoothing out any trapped air bubbles, and seal.

All pickles, fruit sauces, catsups and bottled fruits must be sterilized in the bottle to prevent fermentation. Fill the bottles to within 1 inch of the top, and seal lightly with a cork or screw-top cap. The easiest method is to place the loosely sealed jars in a preheated oven at 300°F for 40-60 minutes, depending on the solidity of the contents, and then screw down lids tightly. A vacuum will form when the mixture cools; but the preserve will not keep quite as long as by the water-bath method. For this, put a trivet in a big pan or line the bottom with a folded cloth. Stand the bottles in place, and fill the pan with water to reach their necks. Let the water boil vigorously for at least 15 minutes; then carefully remove the bottles and secure the cap or cork tightly.

# HOW TO PREPARE INGREDIENTS

The essential ingredients in preserves are sugar and salt, vinegar and oil. Use brown sugar where specified as this gives a distinctive and stronger flavor. For chutneys and sauces, you may find it useful to keep at hand a jar of ginger root preserved in syrup, and a package of candied ginger, too. Spice is, of course, the soul of a good chutney, in the right combination, so your rack should include soft spices — cloves, nutmeg, cinnamon, cardamom — for soft fruits and fiery flavors — chilies, peppercorns, mustard seeds — for piquant preserves.

It is a myth that preserves can be made well with the worst of a crop — in fact, the opposite is generally true. It is the slightly unripe fruit that makes the best jam. Blemishes can introduce unwanted undertones to the flavor, and fruit for bottling or preserving should be at the peak of condition. Try to avoid squashing your blackberries or dropping your apples: once the skin is broken, unwelcome yeasts will start to form.

The old saying *an hour from the garden to the pot* still holds true, even if an hour is rather going it. Aim to give yourself a clear run — a whole afternoon, or evening (many fruits are best picked in early evening), without other distractions. It isn't easy to make a clear jelly and a meal at the same time. And once the sugar is in, think twice before answering the phone!

# JARS & STORAGE

You can rush out and invest in a raft of glass preserving jars with rubber seals, but the essence of country preserving is an abhorrence of waste. The country cook will save jam jars and useful bottles throughout the year, and the eclectic range of shapes and sizes adds to the Ali Baba delight of a well-stocked larder or cabinet. Vinegar-based preserves such as chutneys and pickles begin to dry out as soon as they are opened, so the traditional shape of a chutney jar is tall and thin; jam jars, on the other hand, may be round and fat, perhaps to denote the sugar they contain.

Old stoneware and crockery jars are nice in principle, but dodgy if the glaze is cracked or crazed. French mustard can be bought in wide-mouthed stoneware jars with a big cork. When empty, remove the old wax in very hot water. Sterilize as usual, fill it with your preserve and heat sterilize if necessary, then hammer the cork in tightly and seal by dipping the head of the jar into hot paraffin wax; this effectively prevents any air from reaching the contents.

The quality of the seal is crucial: even oil becomes rancid if exposed to air. A perfectly good way to keep a jar of jam or chutney airtight is to run a spoonful of melted paraffin wax – candle-ends will do – over an initial paper seal. Let the wax solidify, and then repeat the process. If you are

re-using old lids, examine the plastic coating on the inside, and throw away any that are rusted or pitted, for vinegar will eat through bare metal in no time. Lidless jars may be sealed with a proprietary cellophane that shrinks when wet, and secured with an elastic band. A small circle of cotton fabric placed over the top and tied with a ribbon adds a finishing touch. Jams and chutneys make excellent gifts.

Up to the moment that you fill your containers with preserves, sun and air are your allies; from then on your paths diverge. They now look to rot what they've ripened, and you must keep your jars and bottles away from them. Most of the following preserves should be kept dry, in the cool, away from direct sunlight in an old-fashioned country larder. If you must, you can make do with a closet under the stairs, perhaps, or a lower kitchen cabinet: anywhere that is cool, dry and dark will do.

Most home-made marmalades, jams, jellies and chutneys will last for at least 6 months, and many will last a year or more. Unfortunately, storage dates on home-made produce cannot be an exact science, so if you want to be absolutely sure, eat within 6 months. Once the jar has been opened, store it in the refrigerator and eat within 2 weeks. Curds should be stored in the refrigerator before opening.

Pickles, relishes and bottled fruit and vegetables have a much shorter shelf-life of 6 weeks. Once opened, always keep the jars in the refrigerator and consume within 1 week – not usually too difficult!

# PRESENTATION

Once the jars or bottles are sealed and wiped clean, it goes without saying that they should be labeled. Labels can be as plain or elaborate as you like, but should always record the date on which the preserve was made, and a full description of the contents.

Sauce bottles tend to have dull plastic screw-top lids, associated with the manufacturer of the original catsup or sauce, but the bottles can be enlivened if you whittle down a wine cork to fit the hole tightly. Boil the cork, like any other bottle top, for 20 minutes to soften and sterilize it. When the cork is in place, melt some colored wax in a pan, and dip the bottle top into it for a foolproof seal.

Home-made gifts from the kitchen really are valued, as they convey so much more than something you just go out and pay for, and there is no end of fancying up that can go on the outside of the jar. Use scraps of fabric for decorative lid covers, and secure them with colored ribbon tied into a bow. Or melt down a colored candle (see above,) seal the bottle or jar, and press anything embossed — a coin, a butter mold, a brass button — into the wax as it cools, as a formal seal. Turn your labels into works of art with watercolors or crayons, or try pasting on pressed flowers (of the correct season, of course.)

COUNTRY PRESERVES RECIPES

# MARMALADES, JAMS & JELLIES

Pectin and sugar are the requisites for a jam that sets successfully. Fruits high in pectin (cooking apples, blackcurrants, plums, gooseberries and quinces) combine with more sugar to produce more jam; fruits low in pectin (strawberries, late blackberries, cherries and pears) and vegetables use less sugar, and make less jam.

Jellies are clear and translucent; they are best made with tart fruit, such as crab apples and damsons, and may be flavored with herbs. Simmer the fruit until it is soft, then suspend the pulp in a fine sieve lined with cheesecloth to strain into a clean bowl overnight. Measure the juice, add the same quantity of sugar, and boil until set.

It is a good idea to simmer the fruit to a pulp over a low or medium heat before adding sugar, but after the sugar has been added, a vigorous boil tends to keep the color bright and prevents darkening. Once on a boil, jams will set between 10 and 15 minutes. To test for set, use a jam thermometer. As an alternative, place a drop of the boiling jam onto a clean saucer, blow to cool, and push it with your fingertip. If it smears easily across the plate, the jam is still too runny. Boil for a few moments, and repeat the test. As soon as the drop of jam crinkles under your finger, it's ready to pour into jars.

*Seville marmalade*

## Seville Marmalade

*Glut is here the mother of invention; and Mrs. Keiller, whose husband had rashly bought up a shipload of these bitter oranges in Dundee, hit upon this method of using them up.*

2 pounds Seville oranges
5 pints water
juice of 1 large lemon
4 pounds sugar

Wash the oranges, and put them in a large saucepan with the water. Cook over a low heat for about 2 hours, until the peel can be easily pierced with a fork. Take the oranges out of the pan and when cool enough to handle, cut them up, in thick or fine shreds, saving all the seeds. Put the fruit into a preserving pan. Tie the seeds in a cheesecloth bag, and add this to the cooking liquid in the saucepan, with the lemon juice. Boil for 5 minutes. Strain the liquid and add it to the shredded fruit. Boil until the mixture is reduced by one-third. Add the sugar and stir to dissolve; then bring to a boil, and boil fast until setting point is reached. Cool briefly, stir and pour into jars. Seal and label.

## Grapefruit Marmalade

*Marmalades and marmalets were made of citrus fruits long before Mrs. Keiller; this is one made since her death, with the waspish zing of grapefruit.*

3 grapefruit
4 lemons
5 pints water
3 pounds sugar

Peel the fruit quite finely so that as much pith as possible is left, then remove the pith. Set aside the peel and pith. Cut the fruit in half and remove the seeds. Put these with the thick pith from the grapefruit into a cheesecloth bag. Chop the fruit roughly on a plate to save the juice. Shred all the peel finely. Put everything into a preserving pan with the water, and simmer until soft – about 1½ hours. Remove the cheesecloth bag, squeezing out any liquid. Stir in the sugar. Bring to a boil and proceed as for Seville Marmalade.

## Summer Squash, Rhubarb and Ginger Jam

*Vegetable jams are not as unusual as com-*
*mercial producers would suggest. This is a*
*good jam for late summer, when the*
*rhubarb is fat and the squashes are sprawled*
*like stranded zeppelins.*

3 pounds summer squash
3 pounds rhubarb
6 pounds sugar
juice and rind of 3 lemons
¾ cup preserved ginger, chopped

Peel and cube the summer squash.
Strip the stringy fibers from the
rhubarb, then cut the stalks into 1-
inch lengths. Put the summer squash
and rhubarb with the sugar in a large
bowl, cover and leave overnight in the
refrigerator. Pour the contents of the
bowl into the preserving pan together
with the lemon juice and chopped
ginger. Chop up the lemon rind, tie it
in a cheesecloth bag, and suspend it
over the edge of the preserving pan.
Bring the pan to a boil and boil hard
for about 30 minutes, until setting
point is reached. Remove the cheesecloth and rind, pour into jars and seal
and label.

## Gooseberry Jam

*One of the easiest jams to make, as goose-*
*berries have a high pectin content and set*
*readily. If you like a slightly tart jam, then*
*it is also one of the nicest. Unripe goose-*
*berries are best for making jam as their skins*
*are less tough. If you can, cook the berries*
*in a copper preserving pan so that they keep*
*their green color – otherwise they will turn a*
*pinkish-amber shade.*

4 pounds gooseberries
2 pints water
4 pounds sugar

Top and tail the gooseberries. Put the
fruit with the water in a preserving
pan, cover with the lid and cook slowly over a low heat, stirring from time
to time. When the gooseberries are a
pulp, add the sugar, stir until it has
dissolved, then bring to a boil and boil
until set, about 10-15 minutes. Pour
the jam into jars. Seal and label.

*Gooseberry Jam*

## Fig Jam

*Figs are almost mythically gorgeous things, a gift from Bacchus, the Romans said; and unless you are lucky enough to have a tree, then this is a precious jam you are likely to make only in this rather small quantity.*

3 lemons
½ pound cooking apples, peeled and sliced
1 pound fresh figs, roughly chopped
1 pound sugar

Squeeze the juice of all 3 lemons, and pare the zest of one of them. Put the apple slices and chopped figs into a pan with the lemon juice and zest. Cover the pan, and simmer until the fruit is tender. Add the sugar, and stir until it has dissolved. Then boil the jam quickly for 15 minutes, before testing the set. Pour into jars, then seal and label.

*Fig Jam*

## Apple, Lemon and Ginger Marmalade

*Another recipe to make the most of your windfalls.*

5 pounds cooking apples
2½ cups water
juice and finely chopped rind of 3 lemons
4 oz preserved ginger, finely chopped
2 teaspoons ground ginger
4 pounds sugar

Peel and core the apples and cut the flesh into quarters. Put the peelings and cores into a pan, cover with the water and boil for 20 minutes. Put the flesh of the apples into the preserving pan, pour the water from the peelings over and boil until soft, then add the rest of the ingredients. Bring it to a boil again and stir until setting point is reached. Bottle as usual.

## Blackcurrant and Rhubarb Jam

*An unusual and beautifully colored jam.*

5 pounds blackcurrants
1 pound rhubarb
3¾ pints water
7 pounds sugar

Pick the currants off their stems and cut the rhubarb across in short lengths. Put into a pan with the water until the fruit is thoroughly soft, stirring all the time to make sure that the fruit doesn't burn on the bottom of the pan. When the fruit is a pulp, add the sugar and boil fast for 15 minutes but not more, stirring all the time. It should set very quickly. Put in jars. Seal and label.

## Rose Jelly

*This jelly is made from the witchy crab apple and blushing rose. No exact quantities here, but keep the juice to sugar ratio in the proportions given, and you can't go wrong.*

crab apples (see method)
water, to cover
granulated sugar (see method)
rose petals (see method)
superfine sugar (see method)

Wash and cut up the crab apples. Put into a pan with enough water to cover. Boil until the fruit is quite soft. Strain through cheesecloth. To each 2½ cups of juice, add 1 pound of granulated sugar. Boil quickly until the jelly sets. Crush a quantity of strongly perfumed fresh rose petals with superfine sugar (about 2 cups of rose petals to 1 cup of sugar) to a powder so that the sugar absorbs the juice from the petals. Cover with the smallest quantity of water, and stew gently in a covered dish in a preheated oven at 300°F for 1 hour. Strain and add to the crab apple jelly; then bring to a boil. Put into jars.

---

## Mint Jelly
*A staunch friend to lamb in winter.*

4 pounds cooking apples, roughly chopped
5 cups water
white sugar (see method)
24 fresh mint leaves
sprigs of mint for decoration (optional)

Put the apples and water into a pan and simmer until the fruit turns to pulp, stirring frequently to prevent burning, about 5-8 minutes. Strain the pulp through cheesecloth overnight. To each 2½ cups of juice, add 1 pound of sugar. Add the mint and boil until set. Remove the mint leaves, and pour into jars. If liked, add a fresh sprig of mint to each jar as decoration.

## Tomato Jam

*At the end of summer those glassy rows of tomato farms are selling vast quantities of their crop for a song. This is a recipe which evokes the hidden sweetness of the tomato.*

5 pounds ripe tomatoes, peeled and sliced
¼ cup candied ginger, chopped
2 lemons, sliced
4 pounds sugar

Put the tomatoes, ginger and lemons into a preserving pan. Add the sugar. Cook very slowly for 2½-4 hours until quite thick. Pour into jars and seal.

Tomato Jam

37

### Blackberry Jelly

*Nothing is so evocative of fall as blackberry bushes laden with soft black fruit; and no jelly comes so deliciously from the lap of the gods. Here, the jam makers have a decided advantage over idle pluckers: like most fruit, blackberries contain the highest amount of pectin shortly before they ripen, and the early crop makes the most flavorsome jam.*

4 pounds blackberries
2 cups water
sugar (see method)
juice of 2 lemons

Put the blackberries with the water into a pan and simmer for 30 minutes, or until quite soft. Press through a fine strainer to extract all the juice; discard the pulp. Add 1 pound of sugar to each 2½ cups of juice. Put with the lemon juice into a pan, bring to a boil and boil until set. Pour into jars. Seal and label.

---

## Spiced Quince Preserve

*The quince bestows its favors particularly on the preserve-maker as it doesn't make good eating straight from the tree.*

7 quinces, peeled, cored and chopped
water, to cover
grated rind and juice of 4 oranges
grated rind and juice of 1 lemon
2½ pounds sugar
1-inch cinnamon stick

Put the quince into a pan and cover with cold water. Cook until quite soft, adding more water if necessary to prevent the fruit from burning. When tender, press through a strainer. Put the strained fruit into a pan with the grated orange and lemon rind and juices. Add the sugar and cinnamon stick, and bring to a boil. Boil rapidly for 10 minutes, or until the mixture jells. Remove the cinnamon stick, then pour into jars, seal and label.

## Blackberry Cheese

*A fruit cheese is a jam with the moisture cooked out. In the United States the same method is used to produce fruit leather. Pour it into a shallow mold – a teacup, or a soup plate, say – so that the cheese can be turned out whole, and eaten wickedly in slices. Wrap the hot cheese in waxed paper, well pressed down, and seal in cellophane. Store in a cool, dry place for 3 months before eating, then eat straightaway. Serve at room temperature.*

2 pounds cooking apples
2 pounds blackberries
granulated sugar (see method)

Peel but do not core the apples; cut them up roughly. Put the fruit in a saucepan and cook very slowly, covered, until reduced to a pulp. Rub through a coarse strainer into a bowl. Measure the strained pulp and add an equal quantity of sugar. Stir over a gentle heat until the sugar has dissolved, and the mixture has thickened so that a spoon leaves an empty trail behind it. Take great care that the mixture does not stick or burn. Pour the fruit mixture into a mold, and wrap in waxed paper immediately.

## Lemon Curd

*Until you have tried home-made lemon curd, you have no idea how good it can be. Store unopened jars in the refrigerator for up to 1 month. Once opened, eat within 1 week.*

1 cup sugar cubes
2 large lemons
¾ stick butter
3 eggs, beaten

Rub the sugar cubes over the lemons so that they absorb the flavored oil from the skin. Put the sugar cubes in the top of a double boiler. Add the butter. Squeeze the juice from the lemons and add this to the pan with the beaten eggs. Set the pan over barely simmering water and cook, stirring constantly, until the mixture thickens. Pour into jars and refrigerate.

## Dried Apricot Jam

*This jam can be made all year as dried apricots have no season.*

12 ounces dried apricots
3¾ pints boiling water
2 pounds sugar
juice of 2 lemons

Wash the apricots, put them in a large bowl and pour over the boiling water. Once the water has cooled, cover and leave for a day in the refrigerator until the apricots are swollen and soft. Pour the apricots and soaking liquid into a pan and simmer until tender. Add the sugar and lemon juice. Bring to a boil and bubble until the jam sets. Pour into jars. Seal and label.

## Pumpkin Curd

*Store in the same way as Lemon Curd.*

4 pounds pumpkin, peeled and deseeded
½ cup water
4 pounds sugar
2 sticks butter
juice and grated rind of 4 lemons

Cut the pumpkin flesh up into cubes. Boil in the water until tender, then press through a strainer. Put into a preserving pan. Add the sugar, butter and grated lemon rind and juice. Stir well and simmer for 15 minutes. Pour into jars. Seal and label. Store in the same way as for Lemon Curd.

*Pumpkin Curd*

# PICKLES & CHUTNEYS

Cold dishes – ham and beef, cheese and salads – are thinner in flavor than hot ones, and are made memorable by the pickles and chutneys which accompany them. The idea here is to pack a punch of flavor into a small space, with fruit and vegetables bearing a raft of delicious spicy flavors.

The glory of home-made chutney is its versatility: almost anything goes, as long as the proportions are maintained. While the supermarket can offer you a dozen varieties, solemnly adjusted to the public taste, in the kitchen you can combine ingredients like twists on a Rubik's cube. Corral your glut of zucchini and your green tomatoes, and make free with the spices and aromatics you really like.

Pickles and chutneys often have an oriental inspiration – *chatni* is Indian, and ketchup comes from the Chinese *koe chiap*, a pickled fish sauce brought to Europe in the late seventeenth century. Medieval Europeans knew about spices, too. Traded from the Levant, and across the Mediterranean, they made their winter stores good to eat.

In China, brides-to-be would be asked to prove their ability to make good pickles by their prospective mothers-in-law. In more liberated societies as well, men really like pickles.

## Zucchini Chutney

*Chutney can be rather murky, however delicious; but in this recipe it retains a Mediterranean brilliance of color. Use yellow zucchini, if you can; or mix with green. Pumpkins could be substituted for zucchini, in which case peel and deseed.*

5 pounds zucchini
2 pounds fresh, ripe tomatoes, roughly chopped
1 pound onions, chopped
10 garlic cloves, peeled and chopped
2½ pints malt or wine vinegar
1⅓ cups golden raisins
4 tablespoons salt
1 tablespoon each peppercorns, allspice, ground ginger, coriander seeds
3 pounds white sugar

Cut the zucchini into ¼-inch rings, and halve. Put them into a preserving pan with the chopped tomatoes, onions and garlic, 2½ cups of the vinegar, the golden raisins, salt and spices, and bring to a boil, slowly. When the vegetables are tender, about 2 hours, add the remaining vinegar and the sugar, and stir to dissolve. Continue cooking until the mixture thickens, and then pour into jars. Seal and label.

## Gooseberry and Mustard Seed Chutney

*A pale, translucent chutney with a mighty taste.*

1¼ cups mustard seed
1 tablespoon cayenne
2½ pints malt vinegar
3 pounds green gooseberries
2 pounds brown sugar
scant ⅓ cup salt
1½ pounds seedless raisins
1⅓ cups currants
10 garlic cloves, skinned

Wash and dry the mustard seed, and bruise it gently. Add the cayenne to the vinegar. Put the gooseberries, the mustard seed and vinegar into a preserving pan, bring to a boil and boil until tender. Add the sugar and salt, and stir until it has dissolved. Press through a strainer. Mince the raisins and currants. Bruise the garlic thoroughly. Mix all the ingredients together, then boil briefly until the mixture is rich and thick. Pour into jars, seal and label. The longer the chutney is kept, the better its flavor.

*Gooseberry & Mustard Seed Chutney*

*Plum Relish*

## Plum Relish

*A tasty sauce to accompany pork, duck or other rich meats.*

4 pounds plums
2½ cups vinegar
4 cups brown sugar
3 teaspoons salt
4 onions
3 teaspoons crushed peppercorns
3 dried chilies
1 teaspoon cloves
2 teaspoons apple pie spice: ground ginger, cinnamon, cloves, few pinches nutmeg

Wash the plums, and discard any stems. Put all the ingredients into a pan, and cover with the lid. Bring to a boil very slowly and cook over a very low heat for 30 minutes. Leave until cold, remove the onions and press through a strainer. Boil the plum mixture for 5 minutes, then bottle. Heat sterilize (see p.17,) then seal and label. Eat within 6 weeks.

## Date Chutney

*This sweet chutney is relieved by apples, ginger, mustard and cayenne, and makes a good foil for cold lamb and pork.*

2 pounds cooking apples, peeled and cored
2 pounds dried dates
1 large onion
1 teaspoon each salt, mustard, and ground ginger
pinch of cayenne
2½ cups vinegar
1⅓ cups brown sugar

Chop the apples roughly together with the dates and onion. Put into a preserving pan. Add the spices and vinegar. Simmer until tender. Dissolve the sugar in the mixture, then return to a boil and pour into jars and seal.

## Pumpkin Preserve

*Pumpkins are ripe just when some cooks are taken over by that primeval urge to lay down food for the winter.*

1½ pounds sugar
1 lemon, sliced
3¾ cups water
2 pounds pumpkins, peeled, deseeded and cubed
2 tablespoons ginger in syrup, finely sliced

Put the sugar and lemon in a preserving pan with the water. Boil until it makes a thin syrup which will stick to a wooden spoon. Add the pumpkin cubes and boil vigorously for 15 minutes. Add the ginger, and boil for a few minutes. Pour into jars. Heat sterilize (see p.17,) seal and label.

## Spiced Crab Apples

*A recipe that doesn't mask the sharpness of this ancient apple. Eat within 6 weeks.*

4 pounds crab apples
boiling water, to cover
peel of 1 lemon, cut into strips
sugar (see method)
white wine vinegar (see method)
½ tablespoon ground coriander seeds
½-inch cinnamon or 1 teaspoon of ground
  cinnamon
½ tablespoon peppercorns, ground or
  crushed in a mortar and pestle

Wash the fruit. Remove the stems and cut out any blemishes. Put into a pan and cover with boiling water. Add the strips of lemon peel. Simmer until just tender, then strain off the liquid. To each 2½ cups of liquid, add 1 pound of sugar, ⅔ cup of vinegar and 1 teaspoon of the mixed spices. Boil the mixture,

stirring to dissolve the sugar. Add the crab apples, and simmer, uncovered, over a gentle heat until the apples are translucent and the syrup is reduced (about 40 minutes.) Ladle the fruit into warmed jars, and cover with syrup. Heat sterilize (see p.17,) seal and label.

## Blackberry Chutney

*Blackberries have a relatively long season. The first picking makes a classic jam; the second – not so rich in pectin – could make this unusual and delicious chutney.*

1 pound cooking apples, peeled and cored
6 onions, finely chopped
3 pounds blackberries
scant ¼ cup salt
3 tablespoons dry mustard
3 tablespoons ground ginger
1 teaspoon mace
2½ cups vinegar
2⅔ cups brown sugar

Chop the apples, and put into a preserving pan with the onions, blackberries, spices and vinegar and cook for 1 hour. Add the sugar, and cook an additional 2 hours. Press through a strainer, pour into jars, seal and label.

## Pickled Walnuts

*The pickled walnuts will be good to eat in 3 months, and they will keep for 2 years.*

about 100 fresh green walnuts
salt (see method)
water (see method)
For each 2½ pints of wine vinegar,
  ¼ cup whole black peppercorns
  3 tablespoons allspice
  2 tablespoons bruised ginger root

Prick the walnuts with a fork and soak in brine to cover, made of 6 cups salt to each gallon of water, for 9 days, changing the brine every 3 days. Drain,

*Pickled Walnuts*

place on a dish, and leave them in the sun for 2-3 days to blacken. Boil the vinegar with the spices for 10 minutes. Put the blackened walnuts into jars, bring the vinegar back to a boil and pour into jars to cover the walnuts. Heat sterilize (see p.17,) seal and label.

---

## Clear Tomato Relish

*An unusual sharp and spicy jelly to serve with cold meats or on the side of a pilaf.*

3 cloves
1-inch cinnamon stick
3 pounds ripe tomatoes, roughly chopped
3¾ cups water
1¼ cups malt vinegar
3 pounds white sugar

Put the spices in a cheesecloth bag and place in a pan with the tomatoes and water. Cook gently until soft. Remove the spices and rub the tomatoes through a strainer. Add the vinegar and sugar and stir to dissolve the sugar. Bring to a boil and boil until the relish reaches setting point, between 10 and 15 minutes. Pour into jars, then heat sterilize (see p.17,) seal and label. Eat within 6 weeks.

*Pickled Turnips*

## Pickled Cauliflower and Red Cabbage

*The pickle jar works its alchemy on these workaday vegetables.*

1 cauliflower
½ red cabbage
1 or 2 dried chilies
4-5 tablespoons salt
2 pints water
1¼ cups white wine vinegar

Wash the cauliflower, and break it into flowers. Dice the cabbage into thick chunks, cutting in one direction, then the other, without breaking the chunks up. Place alternate layers of cauliflower and cabbage in a glass jar, burying the chili in the middle. Dissolve the salt in the water, and stir in the vinegar. Cover the vegetables with the pickling liquid, then heat sterilize (see p.17,) seal and label. Store in a warm place (for example, near a radiator) for about 10 days, then transfer to a cool place. The pickle should be eaten within 6 weeks. Keep opened jars in the refrigerator, and consume within 1 week.

## Pickled Turnips

*Eat the turnip leaves fresh and make this sharp pickle with their roots.*

2 pounds small white turnips
a few celery leaves
4 garlic cloves, peeled and finely sliced
1 raw beet, peeled and thinly sliced
4-5 tablespoons salt
2 pints water
1¼ cups white wine vinegar

Peel and wash the turnips, then halve or quarter them. Pack into a glass jar with celery leaves and garlic, and a layer of beet at regular intervals. Dissolve the salt in the water, and stir in the vinegar. Pour the vinegar solution over the vegetables in the jar. Heat sterilize (see p.17,) then seal tightly and label. Store for 10 days in a warm place (for example, near a radiator,) then transfer to a cool place. Eat within 6 weeks. Store opened jars in the refrigerator and use within 1 week of opening.

## Cherry Pickle

*Cherries often fall before you can eat them: they arrive at low prices in the stores in season, too. This pickle relies on the crisp texture of whole ripe cherries.*

2 pounds ripe red cherries
I pound superfine sugar
For each cheesecloth bag, pinch of cinnamon,
   pinch of ground mace, pinch grated nutmeg
I¼ cups vinegar

Pit the cherries and layer them in a pan with the sugar, alternately. Between every two layers of fruit put cheesecloth bags of broken cinnamon, mace and nutmeg. Add the vinegar and boil for five minutes. Strain off the liquid into a pan and pack the fruit into hot, sterilized jars. Let the syrup boil until it is thick. Strain, discard the cheesecloth bags and pour the syrup over the fruit in the jars. Heat sterilize (see p.17,) then seal tightly and label. The pickle will keep for up to 6 weeks unopened. Once opened, store in the refrigerator and eat within 1 week.

*Cherry Pickle*

## Pickled Mushrooms

*Mushrooms are mysterious and flighty: their arrival in the wild can never be guaranteed. One year nothing, the next year, an embarrassment. So seize them gladly when they arrive in force, and keep them dried or pickled, as in this delicious old country recipe.*

4 pounds button mushrooms
2 teaspoons salt
vinegar (see method)
2-inch piece ginger root, sliced into
    matchsticks
½ teaspoon mace
1 teaspoon peppercorns
2 oz dry mustard

Remove the mushroom stems, and wash the caps in salted water, then peel off the fine layer of top skin on the caps, using a sharp knife. Put the caps into a pan, and cover with vinegar, ginger and spices. Cover and cook in a low oven, about 275°F, or over a very low heat, at less than a simmer, until the mushrooms are small and soft. Spoon the mushrooms into sterilized, heated jars, and cover with the hot vinegar. Heat sterilize (see p.17,) seal and label. Will keep for 6 weeks unopened; eat within 1 week.

## Dill Pickles

*A German recipe that has powered a billion sandwiches in the United States.*

generous handful of celery leaves
4 pounds small pickling cucumbers
1 heaped teaspoon fresh grated horseradish
several sprigs of fresh tarragon
several sprigs of fresh dill
1 heaped tablespoon of salt for every 4½
    cups cold water

Spread the celery leaves over the bottom of a large jar or stoneware crock, and pack the cucumbers in on top, interspersed with generous tufts of all the other ingredients, especially dill. Dissolve the salt in cold water, and pour the brine to cover the cucumbers, holding them down with a weighted saucer. Cover the jar with a cloth, and leave in a cool place for 10-14 days, when the pickles will emerge glossy and crisp. Refrigerate and eat within 6 weeks.

# Moroccan Preserved Lemons

*A taste of North Africa.*

6 unwaxed lemons
3-4 tablespoons salt
1 teaspoon black peppercorns
2-inch cinnamon stick
½ teaspoon cloves
1 teaspoon coriander seeds
1-2 bay leaves

Cut down the lemons on four sides nearly to the bottom, the quarters still attached at one end, flower-like. Rub salt on the insides, then push them closed again. Pour a tablespoon of salt on the bottom of a preserving jar. Pack in the lemons, pushing them down and sprinkling the spices and more salt between the layers, until you reach within half an inch of the top of jar. Press a bay leaf or two down the side so that you can see them shining through. If there isn't enough juice squeezed out of the lemons as they are packed in to cover the fruit, squeeze another lemon or two and pour in the juice. Seal the jar and leave for at least a month, shaking the jar regularly. The lemons should be briefly rinsed before using them.

# Rhubarb Relish

*For all its homey associations, rhubarb is really an Eastern vegetable, as this Innes family recipe from the nineteenth century bears out.*

2 pounds rhubarb
2 pounds onions, finely chopped
2½ cups vinegar
1 tablespoon salt
3 cups brown sugar
1 teaspoon ground ginger
1 teaspoon ground chili
1 teaspoon ground cumin
1 teaspoon allspice
1 teaspoon black pepper

Cut the rhubarb into short lengths, stringing it if necessary. Put all the ingredients together in the preserving pan and boil until soft. Bottle as usual, heat sterilize (see p.17,) then seal tightly and label. The relish will keep for up to 6 weeks unopened; once opened, store it in the refrigerator and eat within 1 week.

# BOTTLED FRUIT & VEGETABLES

These recipes are probably treasured as much for their appearance as for their flavors, the fruits of summer gleaming out through pellucid liquid of mysterious color. They make very good presents, especially the fruits bottled in intoxicating spirits. Rhubarb, of course, is a vegetable, and only its high acid content makes it suitable for bottling; most vegetables, as a rule, are too low in natural acid to bottle safely, except in the form of pickles or jams, and are best preserved in the freezer. It is the luscious fruits which bottle best – peaches, pears, firm berries, quinces – and whose flavor and texture is actually enhanced by mellowing in syrup.

Syrup is the is the simplest creation in the world. Ordinary white sugar is melted into water by stirring over a low heat, then it is brought to a boil and simmered for a few minutes. This is all that is required. For a subtle, non-alcoholic twist, you may add a little cinnamon or lemon peel to the syrup at the end.

After pouring the syrup over the contents of the jar, shake the jar a little to release any trapped bubbles of air, screw the lid down tight and then unscrew half a turn, to let air escape during heat sterilization (see p.17.) Bottled fruit and vegetables will keep for up to 6 weeks unopened; once opened, store them in the refrigerator and eat within 1 week.

*Bottled Early Rhubarb*

## Bottled Early Rhubarb

*For when rhubarb is still pale and slender.*

1 cup sugar
2½ cups water
rhubarb (see method)

Make a light syrup: Dissolve 1 cup sugar in 1¼ cups water over a low heat until clear. Add another 1¼ cups cold water, and let cool. Cut the rhubarb to the length of the bottles or jars, pack it in tightly, and cover with cold syrup. Screw on the lids, and set the bottles or jars deep in a pan of water. Bring the water to a low simmer (do not let it boil,) and maintain for 20 minutes to sterilize the jars. Remove the jars from the pan and screw down the lids tightly.

## Preserved Quinces

*Preserve the queen of fruits with the prince of herbs.*

3 pounds quinces, peeled and cored
water, to cover
juice of ½ lemon
3 pounds sugar
few sprigs of basil

Peel and core the quinces, and cut into ¼-inch segments with a stainless steel knife. Cover with water, add the lemon juice and soak overnight in the refrigerator in an earthenware pot. Put the quinces and water into a pan. Bring to a boil, then simmer until the quinces soften and turn pink. Remove from the heat for 10 minutes. Then add the sugar and boil hard until the fruit reddens and turns transparent, about 10 minutes. Add a few basil sprigs and pour into jars. Heat sterilize (see p.17,) seal tightly and label.

## Chili Oil

*A simple-flavored oil that gives an oriental dash to hot or cold food. The longer it is kept, the hotter it becomes.*

1 tablespoon dried red chilies
2½ cups sunflower oil

Smash the chilies on a board with a heavy knife or in a mortar. Place in a clean, dry bottle and fill to the brim with oil. Seal, shake well, and store for up to 1 month in a cool, dark place before using. Once opened, store in the refrigerator.

## Peppers in Oil

*Use a few yellow and orange peppers*
*among the more flavorsome red ones —*
*flamenco colors in a big glass jar.*

4 pounds sweet red bells peppers
vinegar, to cover
a few bay leaves
handful of peppercorns
4 garlic cloves, peeled
I teaspoon salt
I tablespoon coriander seeds
olive oil (see method)

Roast the bell peppers until the skins
are black. Remove the skins, and
extract the cores and seeds. Put the
peppers in a bowl, cover with vinegar
and leave to soak for 30 minutes. Wipe
the peppers with a damp cloth. Pack
into a big glass jar with bay leaves, a
small handful of peppercorns, the garlic, salt and coriander seeds. Cover
with olive oil and seal. Refrigerate and
eat within 1 week.

*Peppers in Oil*

*Brandied Peaches*

## Brandied Peaches
*A Christmas present to yourself.*

a little water
4 pounds sugar
4 pounds peaches, halved and pitted
2½ cups brandy

Make a syrup by using just enough water to dissolve the sugar over a low heat. Bring the syrup to boiling point, and add the peaches. Cook slowly until the peaches are tender. Peel off the skins and transfer the fruit to jars with a slotted spoon. Boil the syrup for an additional 20 minutes or so, until it is well-thickened. Stir in the brandy, and pour over the fruit. Heat sterilize (see p.17,) seal and label.

## Berries in Liquor
*There's no need to fuss about quantities, just use what you have.*

rye whisky, Scotch whisky or vodka
sugar (see method)
seasonal berries: strawberries, blackberries, currants, greengages, grapes, etc.
2-inch cinnamon stick
2-inch piece of vanilla bean

Half-fill a huge jar or stoneware crock with the liquor. Stir in sugar until no more will dissolve. Pack in unbruised, unblemished berries, tucking the cinnamon and vanilla into the center. Stopper tightly, and leave in a cool cupboard for 1 month before eating – and drinking. Once the jar has been opened, store it in the refrigerator and consume within 1 week.

## Bottled Spiced Grapes
*Seedless grapes make this recipe extremely easy. Serve with smoked fish.*

1¼ cups vinegar
2½ cups water
3 ounces sugar
1 teaspoon mixed ground cloves, cinnamon and allspice
2 pounds grapes

Boil the vinegar, water and sugar with the spices for 10 minutes and leave to cool. Wash the grapes, picking out any blemished ones, and dry them off before packing into sterilized jars. Cover with the cold spiced vinegar. Heat sterilize (see p.17,) seal tightly and store in a cool, dry place.